DIRTY EAR REPORT #3 /
SOUND, MULTIPLICITY, AND RADICAL LISTENING

ERRANT BODIES PRESS

MOVING THROUGH AFFECTSOUNDSCAPES

ANA PAIS

The relation between sound and affect is one of movement, or rather, on the move. Perhaps not always aware of the process, we perceive sound events and affective moments while they happen and when we live through them. They share a set of features that makes one think they could be thought through together. These features are:

> Permeability of bodies
> Collapse of borders
> Immersive
> Atmospheres
> Modes of knowing
> A perceptual continuum
> Rhythms
> Performative: they do things.

Like the experience of sound, affective experience creates a delicate fabric of rhythms, memories and movements that one can listen to. Both listening and feeling are vibrotactile experiences that collapse the borders between bodies and objects, the individual and the collective, inside and outside, private and public, usual categories to conceive reality. This means that our bodies are permeable to both sound and affect, which challenges prevalent notions of the body as self-contained, autonomous and as the original site of emotions.

To every soundscape there is an affectscape and vice-versa. So, one could speak of soundaffectscape to refer to the felt, vibrating atmosphere of a social space, immersive and surrounding us continuously. One cannot stop listening as much as one cannot stop feeling. That is why sound is experienced as a continuum of vibrations, either listened to or felt through. It flows, it propagates and inhabits spaces we create and experience at the same time. Likewise, our affective experience happens in a continuum of sensations, imprinted on the various layers of the body: sensorial and emotional but also

social and cultural, as all affective experience is informed by discourses, narratives, fantasies, desires and acquired ways of feeling. Affective experience
mediates our contact with the world and sound participates in that mediation
as rhythmic pulse.

Atmospheres of soundaffects can be listened to and felt through. In a
room, in a square, in a church or in a football match, we listen to the affective
qualities of those atmospheres, created and determined by those who inhabit
them as well as by the architecture, the way sound travels and disseminates
intensities, the cultural norms, values and narratives. Thus, we listen to them;
we profoundly listen and feel their vibrations, intensities and rhythms. We resonate with others, with situations or places because we listen and feel the
repeated patterns of vibrations, intensities and rhythms set into circulation.

Lastly, there is an inescapable issue when thinking about sound and
affect: they are both immaterial forces, which have material consequences
on bodies that are the mediums of their passage. Hence, they are performative. They do things: they agitate the body, they pump information through the
blood, and they act upon us and summon us to react. It is because sound and
affect are performative that we must ask ourselves how they determine and
potentiate, simultaneously, our thoughts, perceptions and actions.

This is especially relevant when thinking of social spaces and what
came to be known as Public Affect (the shaping of private experience by social and cultural narratives). In *Cruel Optimism*, Lauren Berlant defines public
spheres as affect worlds, that is, cultural configurations of values and norms
that produce fantasies and desires to which people become attached to by
projecting their lives onto them. Needless to say, these affective projections
result from an ongoing negotiation of what is a common interest of a giv-
en moment and society (2011, 226). The ground of public sphere is political,
where voices speak out to debate and negotiate measures and perspectives
on a common interest (that might not be so common). While minorities usually
struggle to have a voice, politicians can easily take the floor. But what exactly
communicates in political speech and what is actually listened to? Berlant de-
veloped an interesting theory. Making the case for George Bush, who wanted

to speak directly to the people (a case easily applied to other politicians), Berlant argues that what comes across during verbal speech is the transmission of noise as the visceral and empathetic affective atmosphere that keeps the audience intimately connected and bounded to the one who speaks, as well as to his or her ideology (idem, 224-5). Such "politics of ambient noise" (idem) is probably the dominant strategy today if we think of Trump's performative attitude or of Marcelo Rebelo de Sousa's (Portuguese President) closeness to the people, which gave him the title of "president of affects". Thus, to speak directly to the people means to speak to their hearts and/or guts, while excluding reflection and judgment from the public sphere. Berlant further sustains: "The transmission of noise performs political attachment as a sustaining intimate relation, without which great dramas of betrayal are felt and staged" (idem). Thus, affective mediation of the political embeds speech and audience in an affectsoundscape that blurs rational argumentation in favor of a tacit apprehension of feelings. Audiences collectively listen through affective noise sharing a sense of belonging or "the affect of feeling political together" (idem) in a better, more hopeful world.

> How does Lisbon express itself?
> How does the city listen?
> How does the city feel?

In the summer of 2016, massive tourism and gentrification was already a painful reality for Lisbonners. Particularly, that summer was the busiest and the craziest I can recall because not only tourists invaded the city but also it was turned into a construction site. Elections for the municipality were due in the following year so the Mayor of Lisbon decided to rush both necessary and cosmetic changes concentrating them in the same period. It was right at the end of that summer (it was still summer in early October, yes), when tourists and construction works were a preeminent feature of the city's landscape and soundscape, that the sixth Dirty Ear Forum took place. The mixture between foreign languages overheard in our strenuous walks and the intense levels of noise and vibrations of construction work all around the city and, particularly, in the street of Boavista Municipal Gallery, the venue where we mostly had our working meetings, created a high impact atmosphere of vibrant, noisy, dusty tension that generated a permanent discomfort.

Lisbon sounded like this:

Construction works	steps	and then
Construction works	markets	and then
Construction works	trains	and then
Construction works	tourists	and then
Construction works	cobblestone	and then
Construction works	knocking on doors	and then
Construction works	gentrification	and then?

Obstacles to traffic and to people's circulation – caused both by bodies and by structures – were overwhelming and determined the sense of aggression one could feel each time one stepped out of the building. It turned easy and enjoyable walks into anxious and stressful tasks. Clearly, all participants were easily able to negotiate the outside mood but for the two locals it was different. That was not the city I knew and that I am pleased to show hosts around. Yet, the affectsoundscape of the city hit us more deeply than the obvious physical distress. The amalgamation of noisy vibrations and collective bodies of tourists was felt as hostile because it was an overwhelming presence in our surroundings as much as they materialized obstacles to our commutes and practices; likewise, the feeling of anxiety and distress caused by such aggressions was experienced through haptic pressure, high peaks hitting against a background rhythm produced by the working machinery. Either way, there was a sonic-affective bubble that surrounded us completely.

The city resisted. It was silent.

A.

How do objects feel?

How do animals feel?

If there was someone to listen, what would you share?

How do objects listen?

How do animals listen?

If there was someone to feel, what would you share?

Windows break when they resonate in certain frequencies. Machines and electronic devices stop working if one's or the space's electromagnetic fields are too charged. I guess this could be a way of listening. Yet, it is not unheard of that plants blossom when they are spoken to, or that of animal's instinctive feelings of love toward their owners. The most incredible example of listening-feeling, however, is water.

In 1994, Japanese researcher, Dr. Masaru Emoto, started an experiment on water. After freezing it, he observed it through a microscope. At first, he took water from different places (tap water, rivers, lakes); then he exposed the water to words (written and spoken), pictures and music, and observed how different vibrations of those materials created different crystals. The result was astounding: water exposed to positive feelings generated beautiful crystals while water exposed to negative feelings generated disfigured crystals.

If humans being are 70% water, they are radically exposed to feeling the vibrations of words, pictures or music. We listen to affect through our whole bodies, the mediums through which each sound / affect propagates. Furthermore, if trees are 60% to 80% of water they might as well be exposed as much as humans. With animals, there can be a million different cases but I am assuming the same logic applies. Yet, objects pose a different question: sound waves hit solid inorganic bodies which allow them to propagate differently from air or liquid mediums. But do they listen? Is there a different kind of imprint in objects of sound-affect waves? Or a different level of vibratory openness to how it can invade you and be felt within?

B.

How to get people to listen when they are not paying attention?

How to create spaces to inhabit different temporalities?

How can we listen to others?

Create a dispositive to regulate regimes of attention. A theater. It works.

C.

What is allowed to be expressed publicly?

What sounds and feelings can become public?

What can a city express?

The set of questions used to entitle the sections of this text was raised during the Dirty Ear Forum in Lisbon. I listed them in a short text to introduce the exhibition we organized at Galeria da Boavista. Although in residencies or workshops we tend to raise questions rather then find answers, I figured the topics could interestingly organize my thoughts.

D.

How does a cobblestone listen?

How does a cobblestone feel?

Membrane, flow, materiality, resistance

In the production Amazonia, by Portuguese theatre company Mala Voadora (première: 9th Nov 2017, Teatro São Luiz), objects talk back to characters. The piece is a sarcastic satire of Amazonia's massive destruction, which started with Portuguese colonization and has been leading to the total extinction of indigenous populations in Brazil. With a self-deprecating humor, it tells the story of a Western avant-garde artist who is sponsored to travel to distant parts of the planet to make art (a *telenovela*) about pressing matters ... The affectsoundscape is dark, smoky with a sparkle of sci-fi and a scent of light advertising ambient rhythms.

There is a critical distance that stands against corporations and world companies that profit from the savage exploitation of natural resources in Amazonia as the production stages a play inside the play or a fake *telenovela* about a family that represents the colonial neoliberal interests in the region. Yet, laughter is not liberating enough to ease the traumatic reality still happening today, thereby causing some discomfort amongst audience members and theatrical props.

The staging of listening and feeling objects in Amazonia is an interesting aspect to help us think through how objects listen. During the whole show, the table where the family meets for breakfast (a repeated scene with alternate dialogues) violently trembles at two crucial moments of the script. As if an almighty roar, bursting from the center of the earth, the table listens to the family talk and gives voice to the jungle. The first moment happens when one of the characters (the mother) shares her ideas of killing indigenous people faster; she knocks on wood to prevent evil eyes and the table starts to shake. The second moment is right before the unintentional suicide of the father, when he has just announced that the investor's money arrived. The table shakes once more.

Significantly, the table reacts to death. Regardless of their verbal meaning, the words pronounced in both moments carry sonic and affective remains. In the performance, the table listens to the soundaffect vibrations, absorbs them and reflects the vibrations of the earth, of the plundered jungle. Neither the table nor the jungle listen to the soundaffect of death like humans do. The table listens through a shared memory of the jungle, as if still part of the jungle; as if information circulates in its wooden molecules reminding it of the repetition of actions of humans throughout the centuries. Wood is the medium through which sound propagates and affect rebounds. Wood is the memory of a tree.

E.

How does a city rhythm us?

While I write these lines, I am still surrounded by an affectsoundscape of construction works as there are several buildings being remodeled next to the street where I live, in the center of Lisbon. From my window, I can see five cranes further downtown. The city as an open construction site is a productive metaphor to think about how we want it to change and how we want to live together. Machines turn over the ground, sturdy blocks of concrete rise up, new facades recover old buildings to give birth to hotels in every corner, where before there used to be traditional commerce.

Rui Costa said: the city is an epidermis with open wounds

TTTTRRRRRRTTTTTRRRRRRRTTTTTTTTTTRRRRRRRRTTTTTRRRRRRRR
TTTTRRRRRRRTTTTTRRRRRRRRTTTTTTTTTTRRRRRRRRTTTTTRRRRRRRRR
TTTTRRRRRRRTTTTTRRRRRRRRTTTTTTTTTTRRRRRRRRTTTTTRRRRRRRRR
of machinery working, startling rhythmic
klanklanklanklan klanklanklan klanklanklanklan klanklanklank klanklank
of carry-ons dragged on the cobblestones, the inner breaking thud
of materials coming down the plastic pipes, the unpleasant laughter
ahahahahaahahahaahahahaohohohohohohohohohohohohohoho
ahahaahahahaha
of tourists in previously quiet streets that hits your intimacy, the
encompassing buzzing coming from several directions at the same time
TTTTRRRRRRTTTTTRRRRRRRTTTTTTTTTTRRRRRRRRTTTTTRRRRRRRR
TTTTRRRRRRRTTTTTRRRRRRRRTTTTTTTTTTRRRRRRRRTTTTTRRRRRRRRR
TTTTRRRRRRRTTTTTRRRRRRRRTTTTTTTTTTRRRRRRRRTTTTTRRRRRRRRR
RRTTTTTRRRRRRRRTTTTTTTTTTRRRRR
TTTTRRRRRRRT

This affectsoundscape excavates a space of enclosure. It is infused with a sense of vulnerability toward an encompassing envelope of sound felt as pressure on the body, which has consequences. I feel the need to protect myself. I hesitate opening windows – to keep sound and dust away – I wake up with the sound of machinery, I avoid going out or taking certain routes. Feeling squeezed in a saturated cloud of omnidirectional sounds. Sounds distribute a sense of non-belonging to places I have known all my life but that have been persistently pillaged (parking places, apartments, esplanades, belvederes, etc.).

The city rhythms us in a contaminated fashion, dirtied with the pace of business and construction: it transmits noise. Differently from political speeches, as Berlant suggests, noise amplifies the dreadful feeling of the city's gentrification, a circulating affective atmosphere that permeates living spaces building up either a sensorial enclosure or a sensorial breakaway. Noise is not an affective atmosphere that comes across as a gut-message from the city. Instead, it is the actual sound of a silent but excruciating pain that destroys attachments. One could say, the city is taking up the soundscape, speaking its viscera out to protect itself.

Beware: Lisbon shakes too.

Bibliography
Berlant, Lauren. 2011. *Cruel Optimism*. Durham: Duke University Press.
http://www.masaru-emoto.net/english/emoto.html

POINTS OF LISTENING

TAO G. VRHOVEC SAMBOLEC

Notes on:

– synchronicity of the unheard

– ambiance

– ground

– silent volumes

– underground

Listening in the intersection between the unheard audible
and the heard inaudible

(a body is formed)

<u>Synchronicity of the Unheard</u>

A human body is moved by the sound waves just like everything else that surrounds it – the ground, the dust on the ground, the wall, the house, the fly buzzing around, the piece of garbage on the floor, the chair, the table, the device, the book, the stone, the fruit, the pen, your hair.

Weak yet persistent sonic vibrations are setting into synchronous motion the molecules of everything they reach. For a short-lived moment these minuscule vibrations indiscriminately perform an involuntary dance of molecules in the air, in gases, in liquids and in solid matters. Yet, with our ears we perceive only a portion of these vibrations, their reflections and the resonances they activate.

What we hear we call sound.

<u>Ambiance</u>

Ambiance engulfs us. We are immersed in it, sensing it continuously with all our senses. Ambiance evolves in an empty space between the solid structures of built environment, ground, sky and the activities taking place. It is ephemeral, airy, transparent, immaterial and transitory. It is "imperceptibly in the foreground", affecting us without being noticed. We are always a part of an ambiance. Our individual movements, attitudes, appearances, voices and mental states radiate through atmosphere, fusing into an overall ambiance of the space. Therefore we are active agents of the ambiance that engulfs us. Being a result of countless human and non-human activities in a place, ambiance makes us behave in a certain way. Our behavior in turn reinforces the mood of that ambiance. Where does the initial mood originate? Is it communal, is it subjective, is it imposed or is it self propagated?

In his paper *A Sonic Paradigm Of Urban Ambiances* Jean-Paul Thibaud describes ambiance as follows:

"[Ambiance] questions the idea of a clear distinction between the perceiver and the perceived, the subject and the object, the inside and the outside, the individual and the world. [...] ambiance enable us to emphasize the 'in-between' and the 'in-the-middle', and through them a relational thought can develop."

Perhaps this "in-between" is a relation that ambiance has with itself. A moment or a duration, an event or a constellation between one or many, living or not, active or passive. Not being fixed to a place or time, this relation can occur between any of the elements at any moment, noticed or not.

Perhaps this "in-between" is the moment when the ambiance hears itself.

Perhaps this "in-between" is another way of saying that the ambiance hears itself.

<u>Ground</u>

Ground as surface
Ground as point of contact
Ground as territory
Ground as margin of visibility
Ground as condition
Ground as possibility
Ground as resistance
Ground as limitation
Ground as stage
Ground as vibrant matter
Open ground
Ground as medium
Ground as construction
Ground as membrane

What is taking place above and on the ground is sending weak shockwaves through the solid matter down below. Inaudible to our naked ears, these shockwaves are vibrating the earth, exciting molecules in stone and asphalt or resonating in built caverns, chambers, parking lots or canalization tunnels below the surface. Always in touch or less than a step away, this space remains inaudible, invisible and inaccessible to us.

Listening to the sound of the ground recordings I have just made in front of the Boavista Municipal Gallery by placing two contact microphones on the asphalt and weighing them down with two cobblestones, you said:

"It is a good concept, ..."

In the silent pause, after the word "concept" I heard your silence speaking:

"But it is too loud, I can not think while it is playing. Can you please stop it?"

Even though the sound of the speaking silence was not propagating through the air, (and the molecules were not performing the dance of these words) I heard the unspoken words sounding with the same loudness and intensity as the sound of the ground recording that was coming out of the loudspeakers.

When I try to recall the loudness of the ground recording I can not remember it. On the other hand, whenever your unspoken words come back to my mind they sound in my inner hearing with the same loudness and intensity as they did when I heard them for the first time – as if this memory transforms me into the volume of the sound of your unspoken words that only I can hear.

Underground

In the Aljube Museum which is dedicated to the resistance and freedom movement during the military dictatorship in Portugal, a regime that was in power from 1933 – 1974, there is a curious installation on display: a desk on top of which there is a typewriter in a half opened wooden box. In front of the table there is a chair with a real size sculpture of a sitting person that is "using" the typewriter.

The box of the size of a small suitcase has two holes on one side that are big enough for the hands to pass through and reach the keyboard of the typewriter. On the topside of the box there is a rectangular glass window making the keyboard and the inserted paper visible when the box is closed. The inside of the box is carefully cushioned with a thick layer of felt. The design of the box allows using the typewriter even when the box is closed, which drastically reduces the loudness of the sound that is produced when the typebar hits the ink tape, pressing it against the surface of the paper with great velocity which is required to produce an imprint of the letter on the paper.

It was explained to me that such typewriters in boxes were used by the resistance movement in order to write letters, pamphlets and communication materials, fearing that the sound of the typewriter will propagate through the walls where it might be heard by the neighbors, who could, if questioned by the police, indicate that they have heard the sound of the typewriter behind the wall. Such indication would be enough to raise suspicion, which would certainly lead the police to search the apartment on the other side of the wall.

What were they afraid of?

Concentration, articulation, contemplation, questioning, reasoning, imagination, doubt, poetry?

Suspicion and fear are recognizing the activity of writing in itself as signaling presence of potential disobedience, turmoil and danger.

Danger of writing as an act of stepping out of time, out of the causal reasoning, out of the transparency of the obvious and the expected, out of the physical determinacies, out of the prescribed outcomes of power relations and operations.

Danger of writing as a silent pause, as a halt that is at the same time a leap and a transgression.

Danger of writing as a creative act that is forming volume to be shared by many (no matter what this volume is expressing), trespassing from the intimacy and privacy of the inaudible inner thought into the public sphere of the heard.

The volume that can be silently amplified to excite powerful resonances in the reading bodies and setting them in motion. The volume that is oscillating between the heard inaudible and the unheard audible, between potentiality and activity, between the underground, the ambiance and the ground, between presence and absence – elusive and irrepressible in its weak power.

LISTENING TO DISINTEGRATION:
THE SOUNDS OF SMOKE
(OR ONE HOUR, THREE MINUTES AND 36 SECONDS, AND THEN SOME MORE...)

DEBORAH KAPCHAN

Initially, William Basinski's ambient, avant-garde composition *Disintegration Loops* gave me a feeling of nausea. Was it because as soon as I pulled the album cover up on Spotify the images of burning towers announced themselves on the screen? Was it this, coupled with the hissing, crackling materiality of a magnetic tape in a state of disarray – the sound impure, the tempo uneven?

Basinski's piece was in a sense accidental. He was trying to digitize an early recording of one of his compositions. However in the process, the magnetic tape literally fell apart. What caused the "disintegration" was the detachment of the ferrite (iron oxide) in the tape from the plastic backing. The disintegration, in other words, was based on a divorce of previously alloyed materials: metal and plastic. The fraying tape produced a repetition, but the erosion was uneven; the loop entrains, but then hesitates unpredictably. Basinski reworked the piece, adding reverb, and finished it on the day of the 9/11 attacks, a day of elemental and social disintegration. It subsequently became the soundtrack of national trauma.

I began to get a headache.

Listening to Basinski is, for me, a decision to linger in the space of discomfort. While 9/11 was an event that punctuated history, *Disintegration Loops* takes us into another temporality, a longer duration, a slower violence. But let's return to the image. It is not the Twin Towers portrayed on the album cover after all, but a lot of billowing smoke in a skyline not immediately recognizable (to me) as lower Manhattan. The smoke itself is in the shape of a butterfly – dense but diaphanous, animal-like, a kind of ephemeral memorial to those falling out of the sky, those falling through the rising smoke that is eclipsing the view of the crumbling towers.

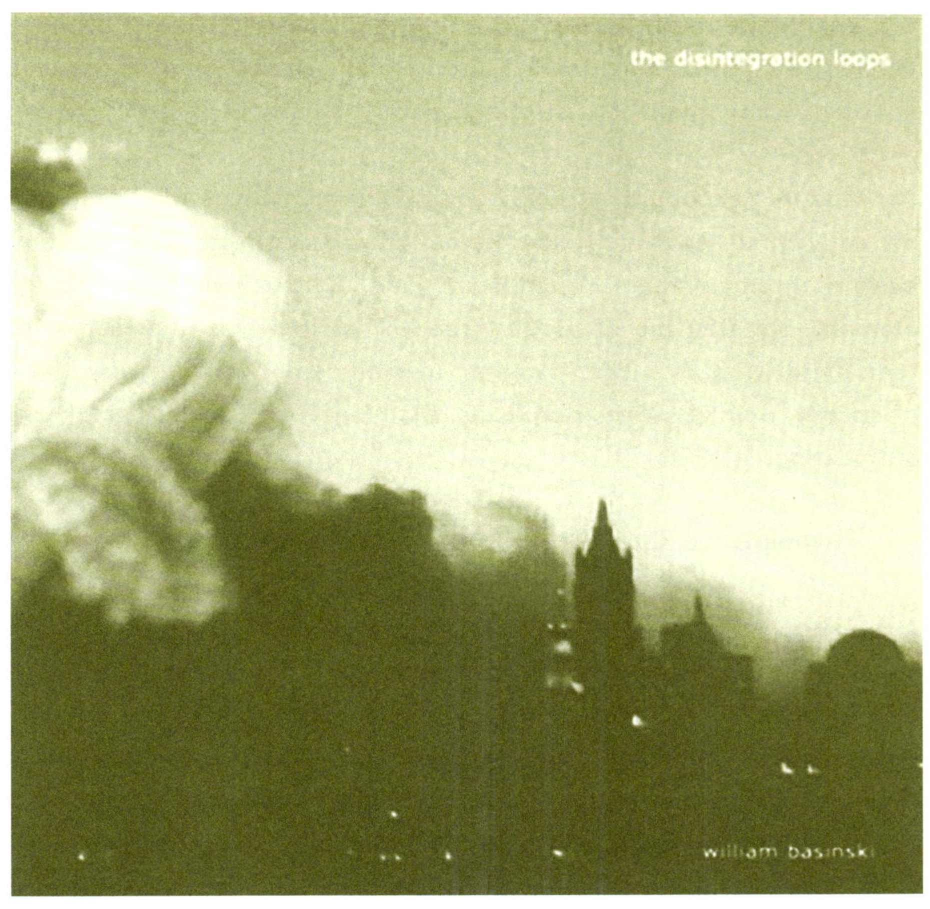

What is smoke made of?

And why does it, being partially solid, float?

How long must I listen to this?

One hour, three minutes and 36 seconds of "remastered"

disintegration.

"Smoke is a collection of airborne solid and liquid particulates and gases emit-
ted when a material undergoes combustion or pyrolysis, together with the
quantity of air that is entrained or otherwise mixed into the mass. ...Smoke
is an aerosol (or mist) of solid particles and liquid droplets that are close to

the ideal range of sizes for Mie scattering of visible light. This effect has been likened to three-dimensional textured privacy glass ... — a smoke cloud does not obstruct an image, but thoroughly scrambles it."[1]

Perhaps this accounts for my nausea; my brain waves are being scrambled, my body/mind "entrained" like the air when it is mixed into the promiscuous skew of three elements – solid, liquid, gas. Smoke, caused by fire, the fourth element, agitates the previous three and incites and rouses the fifth – aether, spirit (what is called "akasha," in Hinduism – which is also the medium of sound). Smoke invites perplexity. *Disintegration Loops* is smoky. And I am suffocating.

What is the sound of smoke?

A nauseous headache is different than a migraine, located somewhere between the sides of the head, the trachea and the stomach. What produces this malaise? For Sartre, it was precisely the experience of being between elements. He talked about it in terms of viscosity. And viscosity – something not solid, not liquid – produces an instability in human perception that has a bodily equivalent: nausea. "Smoke [in order] not to think," Sartre says. "If I could keep myself from thinking! I try, and succeed: my head seems to fill with smoke . . . and then it starts again: 'Smoke ... not to think ... don't want to think ... I think I don't want to think. I mustn't think that I don't want to think. Because that's still a thought.' Will there never be an end to it?"[2] (*Nausea*, p. 99).

(Of course Sartre is talking about smoking a cigarette. Remember that weird moment in history when inhaling tobacco leaves wrapped in bleached paper was something sexy? When bringing smoke into the lungs in one form, and pushing it out the nose in another was a way to suspend not just the breath, but thought itself in a sensual-temporal delay? "... my head seems to fill with smoke ... and then it starts again: 'Smoke ... not to think ... don't want to think ...'")

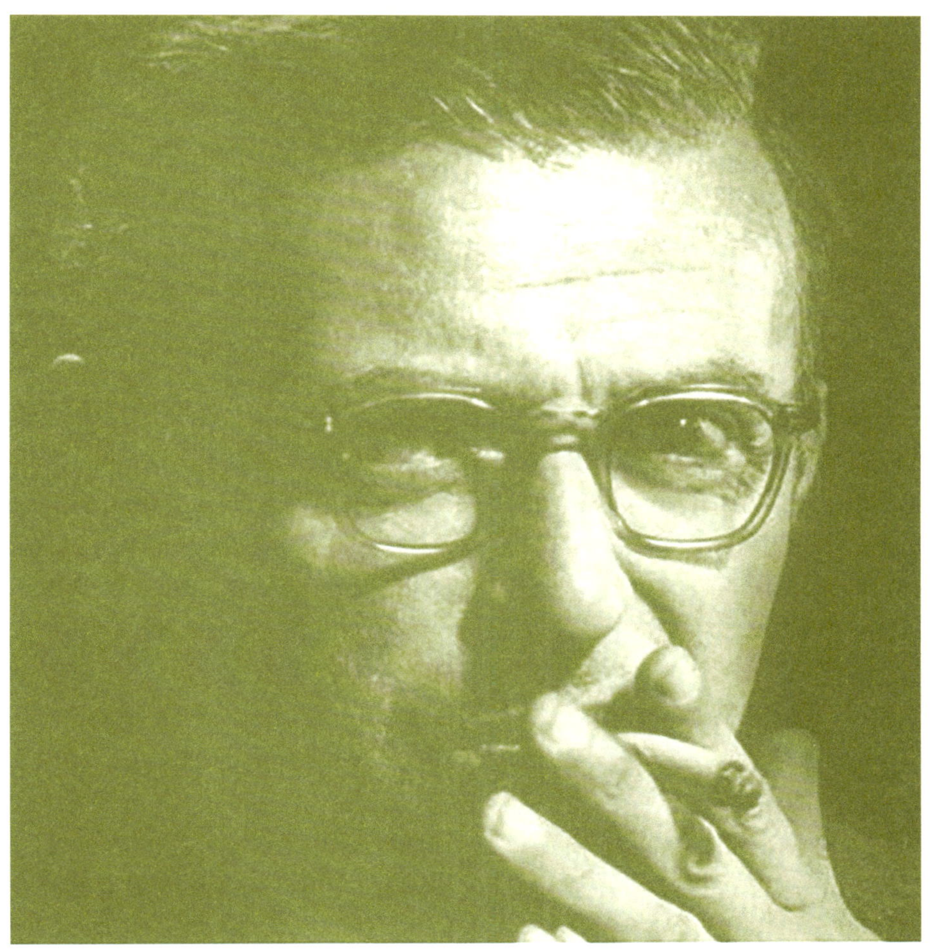

Perhaps smoke does obliterate thought. Perhaps, like physical pain, smoke obliterates language itself.

Following Vygotsky, children do not actually "think" until they have the words to do so, and then their thoughts are constructed in the inter-space of the parent-child relationship. Children's thoughts are necessarily populated by the thoughts of others. The road from co-thinking to inner thinking and subjectivity is one built on words (for Vygotsy), but once achieved, these words also belong to others. "Will there never be an end to it?"

At 24 minutes and nine seconds I pause the piece. I need a break, need to come up for air. Lingering in the space of discomfort has its limits at physical thresholds for pain.

Smoke.
Elements in unusual proximity one to another.
A chemical re-arrangement.
A shock treatment to the brain.
Basinski composed music with smoke loops.

Is it the half-step interval of the two primary notes – G and A flat – that creates this malaise? Is it the echoes of what sounds like a French horn playing a fifth, then a sixth, then a third above the tonic? Is it the forest of thick electronic mesh that underlies the entirety? And if not (only) the intervallic effects, what of the texture? The timbre? That electrical grid of the soul?

And we should not forget the Mie effect – the effect of light meeting particles. "Smoke is an aerosol (or mist) of solid particles and liquid droplets that are close to the ideal range of sizes for Mie scattering of visible light." Mie scattering produces the magnificent chromaticism of sunsets, the orange and reds that suffuse the New York skyline in summer dusk. It is only smoke that makes light bearable at all to the human eye.

But then sometimes the smoke is too thick.

As the piece continues, the attack notes begin to sound like actual attacks – not the pressure of fingers on a keyboard, or the attack of a tongue on a mouthpiece, but explosions in the distance, the sounds of war.

And then everything gets smokier, as if we were inhabiting the head of a soldier listening to gunshot, listening to bombs, listening to the internal echoes of these noises in his head, in ours. [55:16]

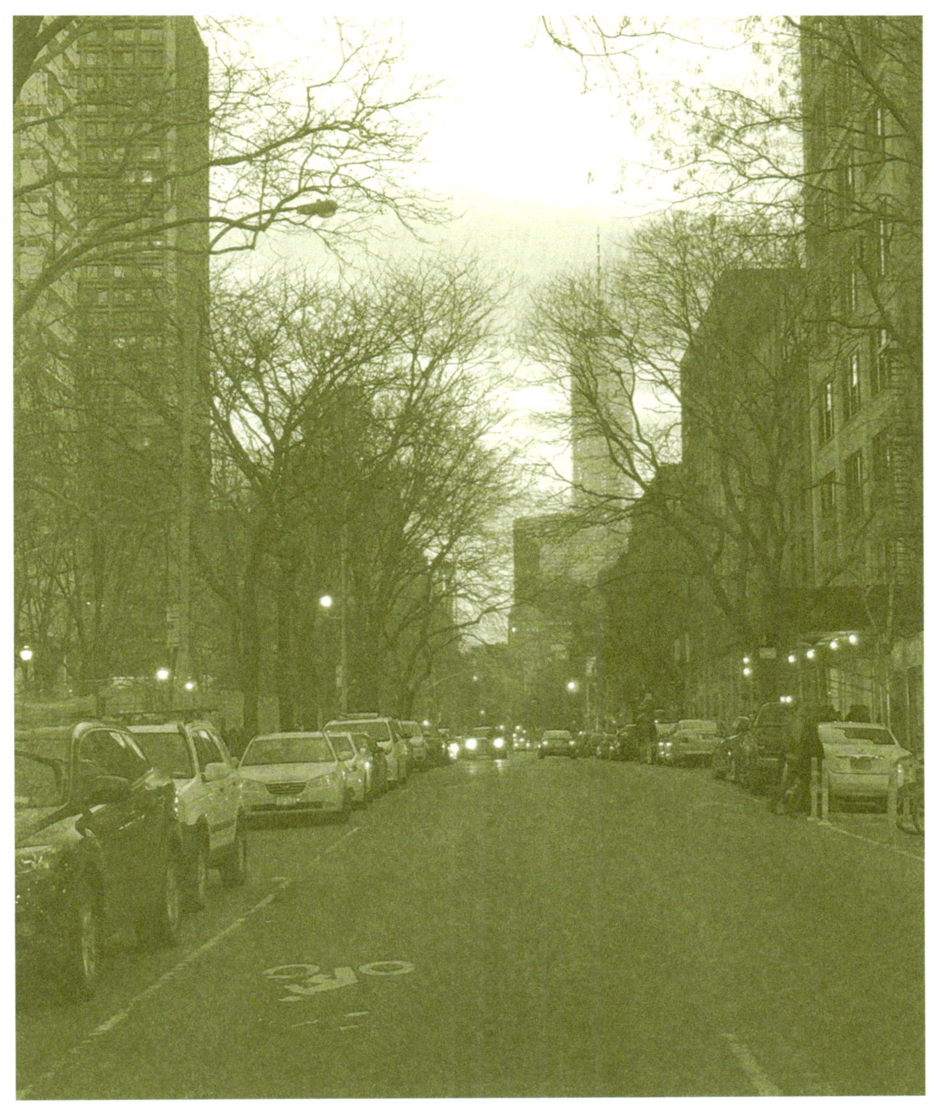

And then the electrical buzz, like fluorescent lights over an electro-cardio-graph machine in an Intensive Care unit [62:21] until we imagine we hear an-other bell-like melody in the distance, calling us to a light.

Buzz, Fade out, Death

<u>CODA: The Distintegration Loops 2.1</u>

But is there life after death, a transmigration of souls in smoke?
A transformation of smoke into clouds?
Is there singular life after listening?

In *The Disintegration Loops 2.1*, which is only ten minutes and fifty seconds long, we hear another aesthetic – this time a more reed-like sound billowing like smoke proliferating. It is the butterfly beginning to take wing. Not fifths this time, but a harmonic series built on thirds, where the tonic and a second enter, like steps into the clouds. It is a more angelic yet metallic reverberation, a gong penetrating the body in all its pores.

Consider some other definitions of smoke: to "fumigate, cleanse, or purify by exposure to smoke"; or to "Subdue (insects, especially bees) by exposing them to smoke."[3]

Fumigation was synonymous with perfuming in the late Middle Ages. And of course smell, like sound, permeates our being, invading and also transforming our very chemistry.

From viscosity to porosity, human vulnerability has a sound.

<u>Conclusion: Listening to Disintegration</u>

Listening subjects are open subjects. When we decide to listen, as I did to Basinki's piece, we are intentionally opening ourselves to an experience of discomfort (in my case nausea), and we are lingering there (one hour, three minutes and 36 seconds, and then some more...)

Lingering in the space of discomfort is an ethical stance that breathes in the smoke that, like ritual incense, changes the brainwaves, voluntarily admitting a certain toxicity into the human body in pursuit of another kind of knowledge – an experiential knowledge, a sound knowledge.

Lingering in the space of discomfort is homeopathic.

Such lingering in smoky spaces, however, is not always a decision. It is more often an imposition. And then the response is to run for one's life. Or to jump to a purer, more rarified atmosphere. Indeed, before people are burned in fires, they usually die of smoke inhalation. It is elemental. Lungs can only filter so much particulate matter.

On the other hand, as we watch and listen to disintegration we imbibe a small part of what will eventually overtake us: the perplexity of smoke in which solids rise instead of fall into the unbreatheable yet unavoidable smokiness of being. Lingering in the smoke, just like listening to disintegration, is an exercise in being-with what is completely foreign and yet profoundly intimate. Nausea. Smoke. Disintegration. Is there singular life after listening?

1. https://en.wikipedia.org/wiki/Smoke, accessed March 9, 2016.
2. Sartre, Jean-Paul. 1964. *Nausea*. Translated by Lloyd Alexander, Introduction by Hayden Caruth. New York: New Directions.
3. http://www.oxforddictionaries.com/us/definition/american_english/smoke, accessed March 28, 2016.

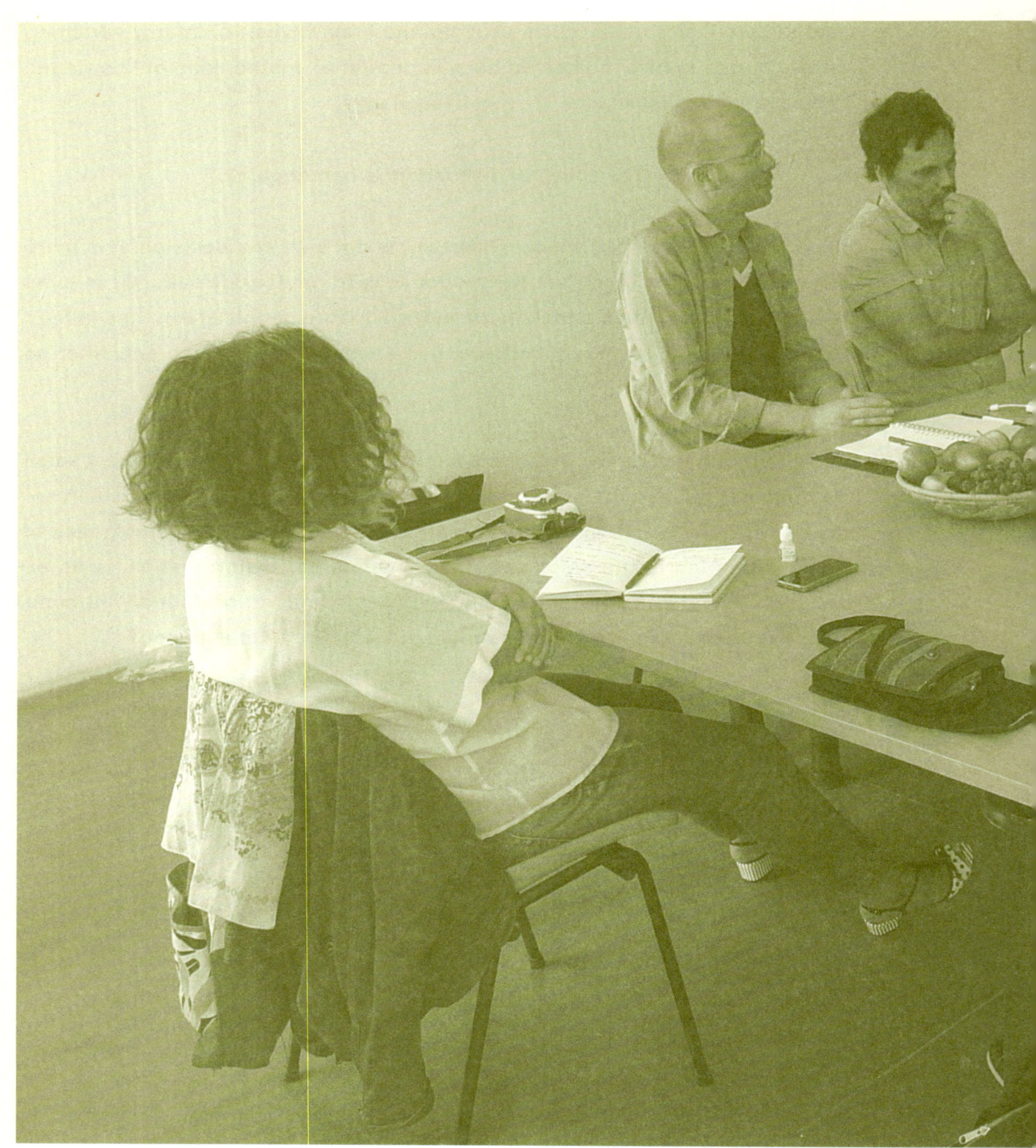

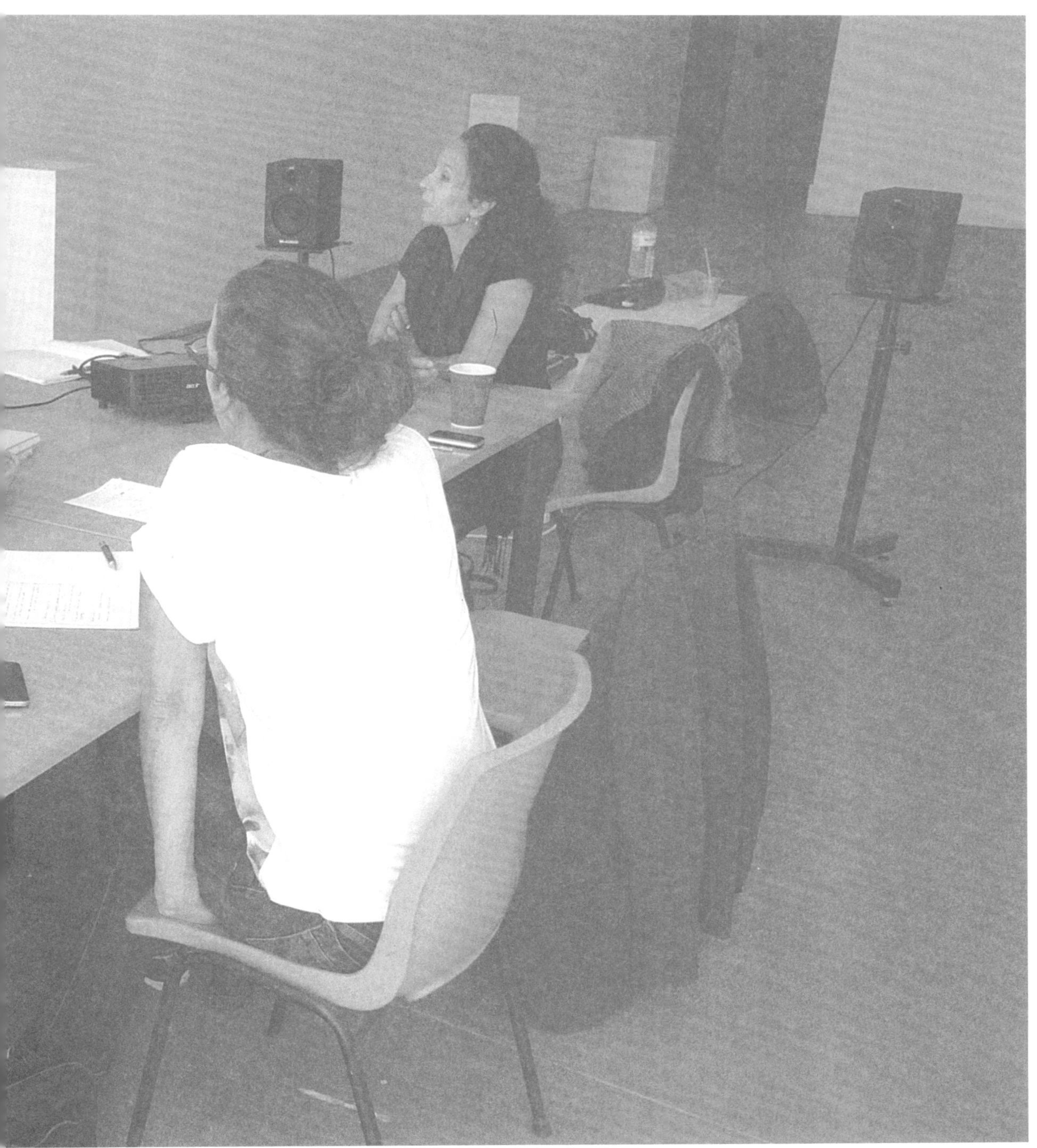

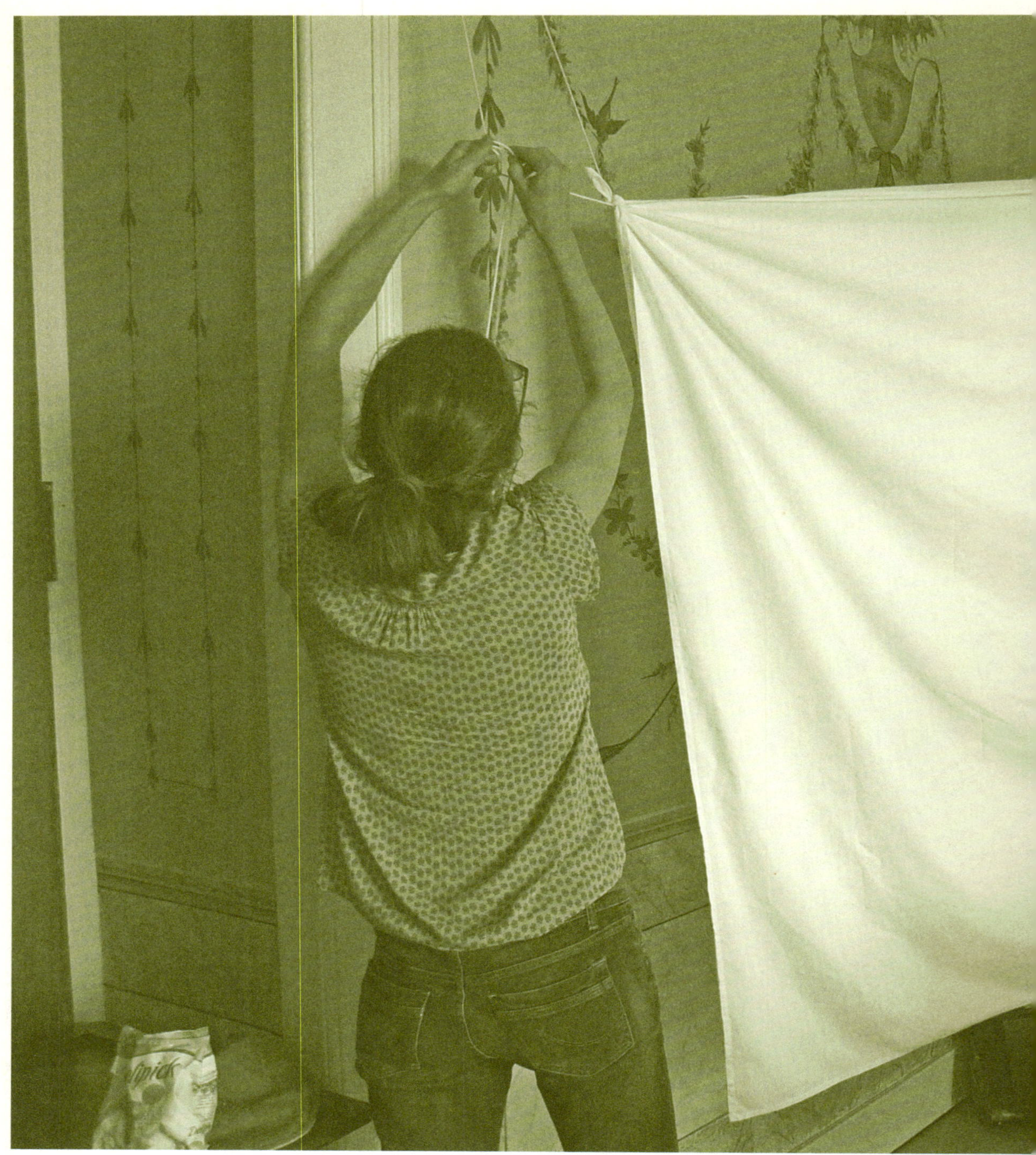

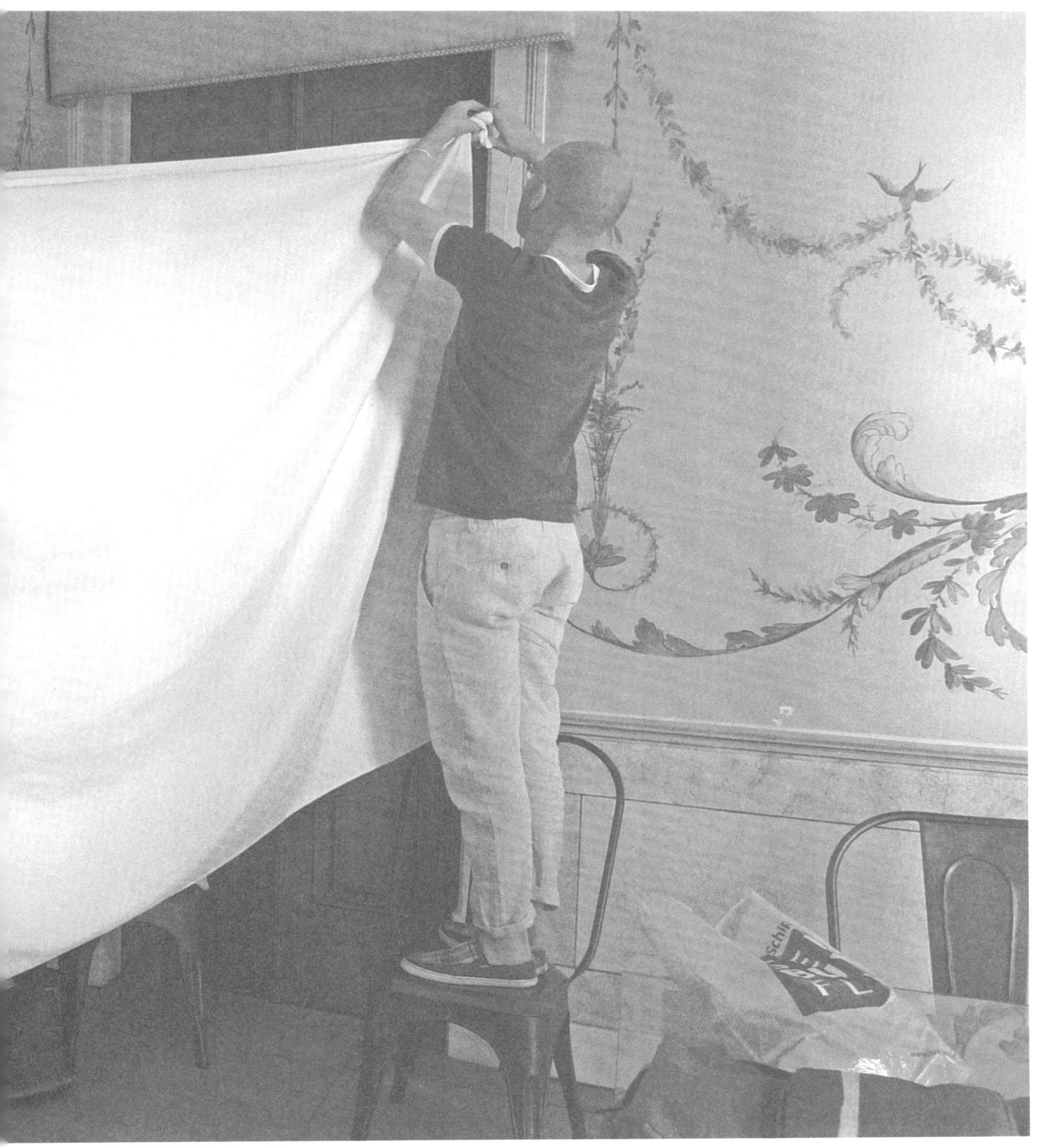

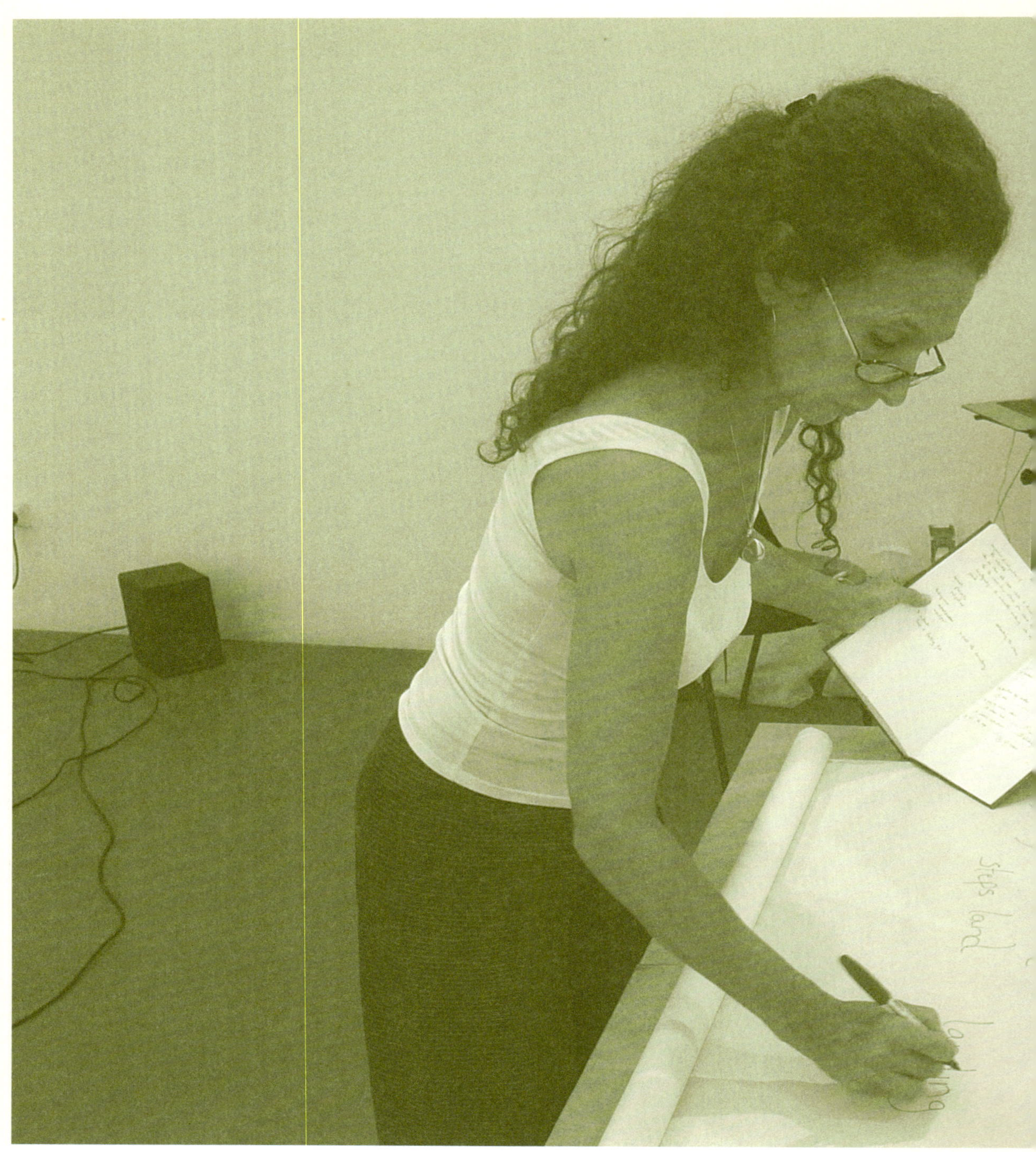

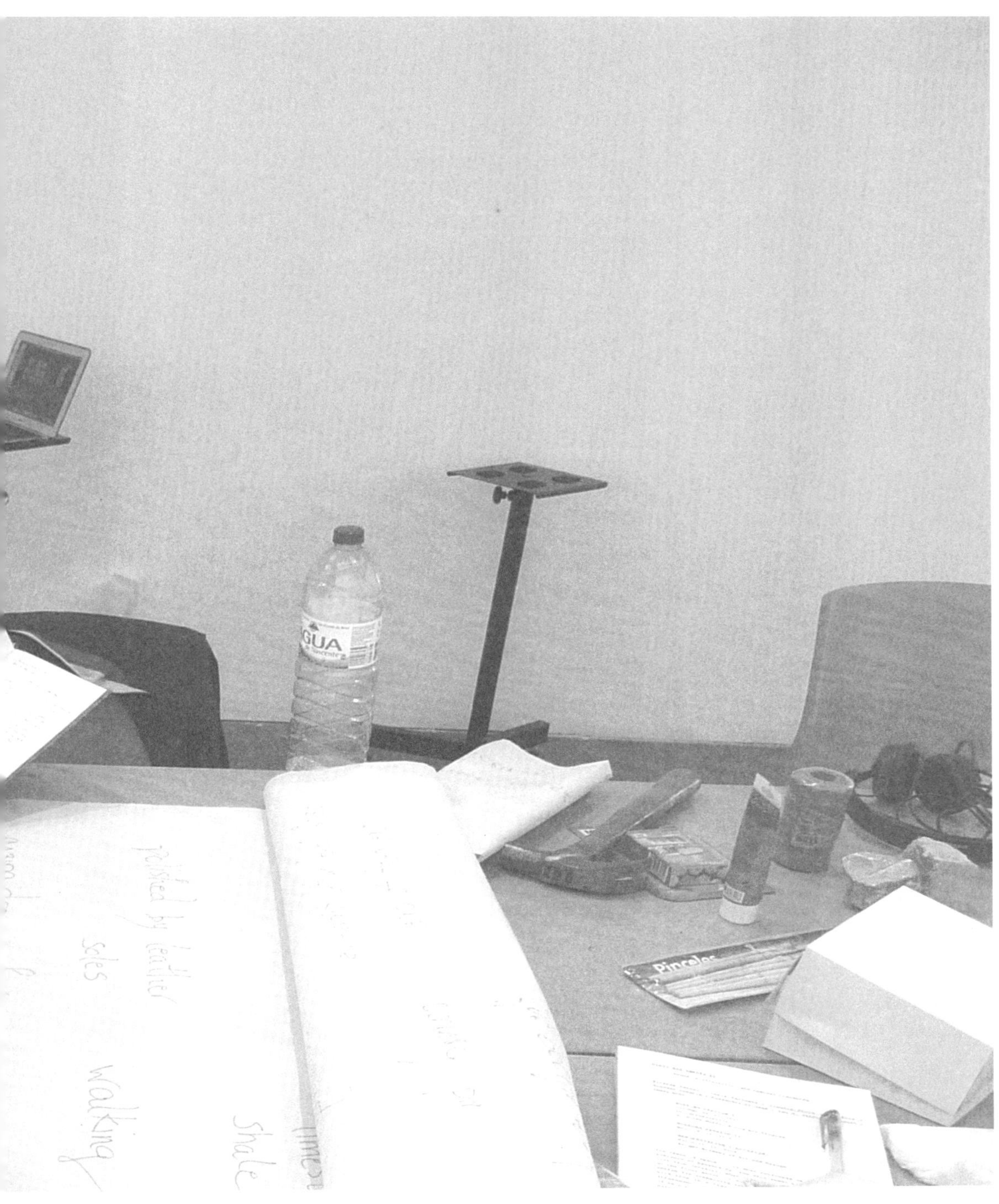

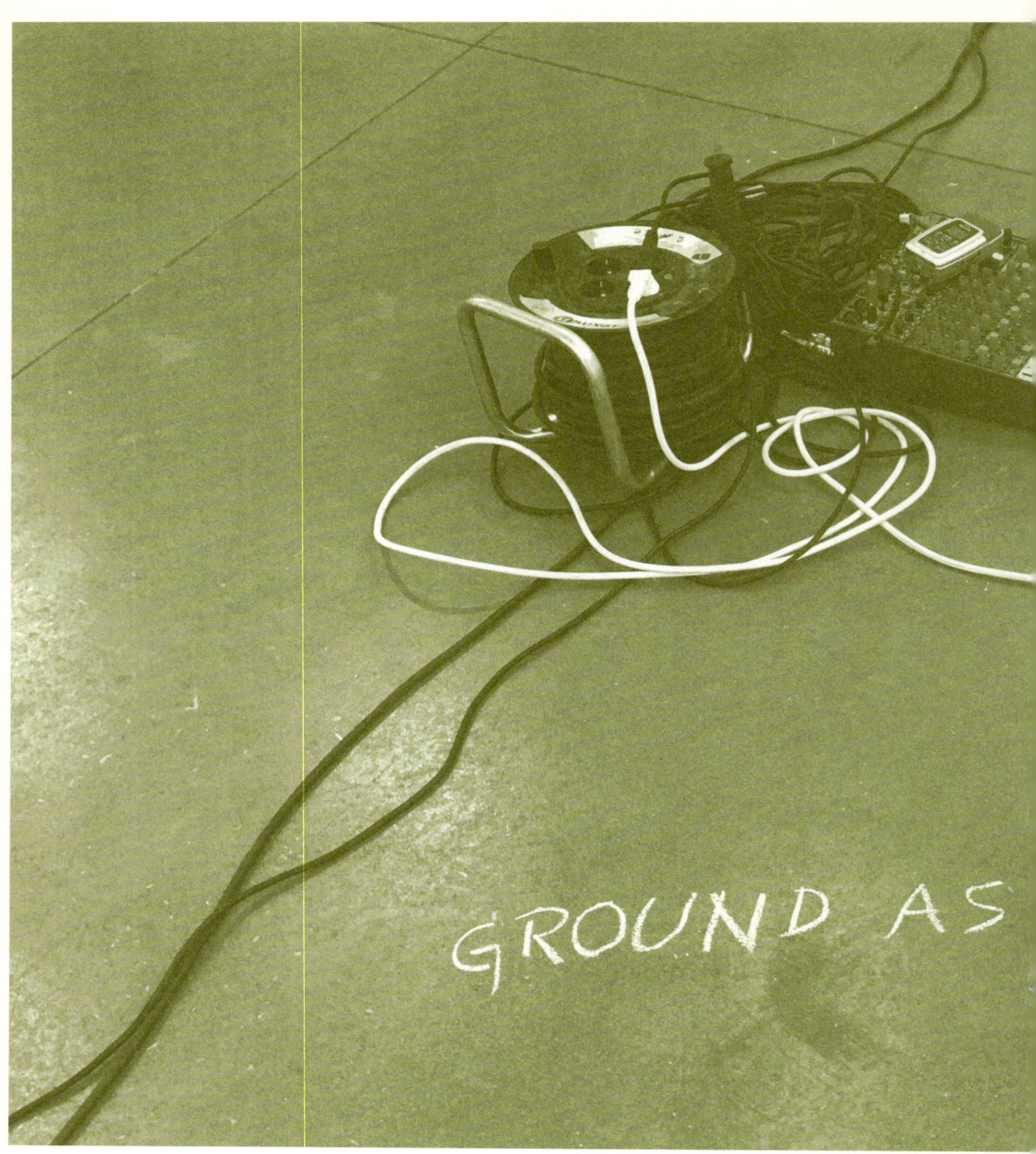
GROUND AS

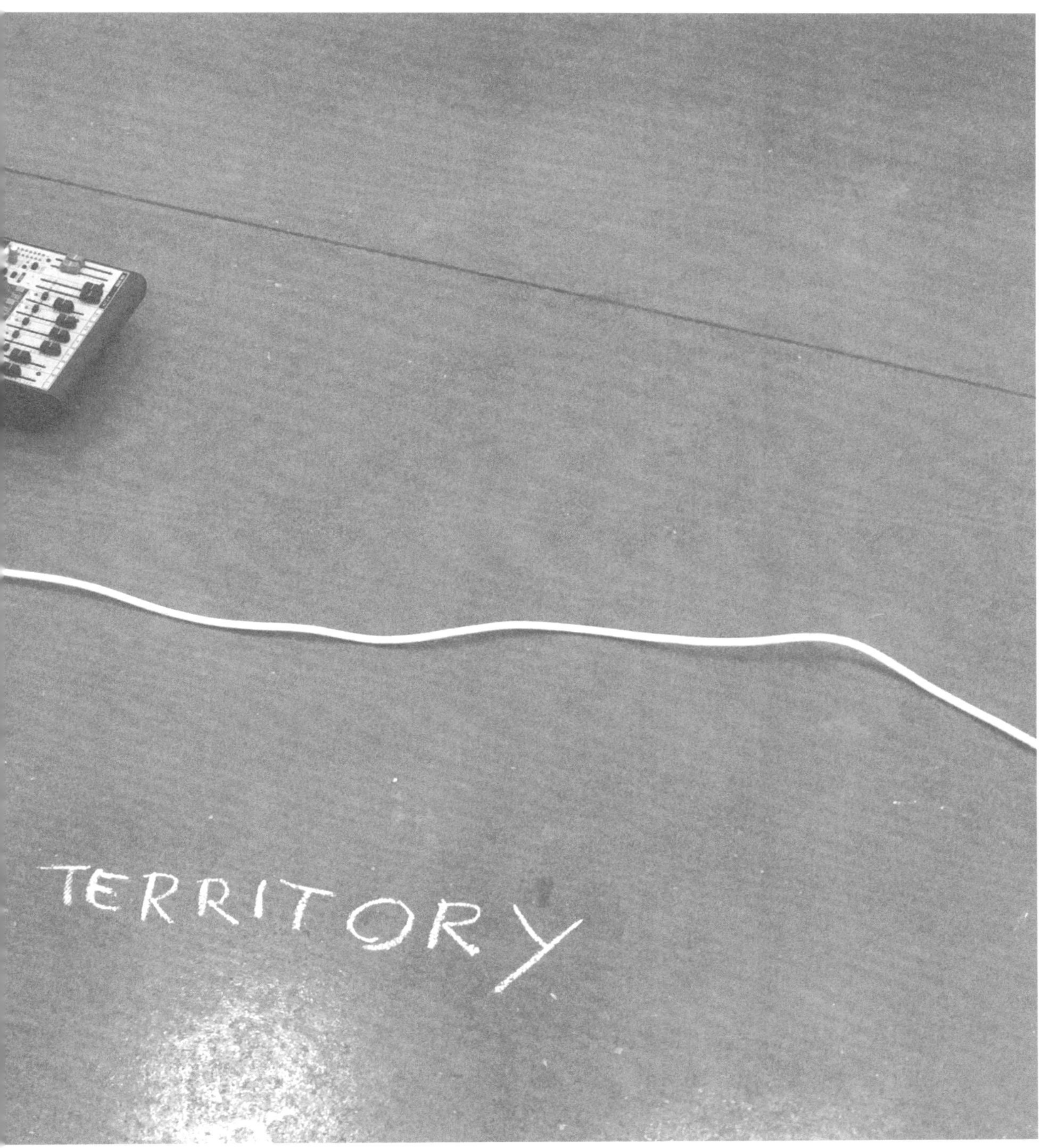
TERRITORY

SELFPORTRAIT FOR SIX VOICES AND A CITY

MARIA ANDUEZA

I have always been curious about the notes that each of us takes while listening to others. As listeners we select and differentiate words and expressions that we collect in a notebook or in single sheets of papers. From that moment the written words remain then forever separated from the voice and the discourse. Conversely, these same words written preserve the connection to some remembrance of the bodies talking and transferring emotions, and emphasis on the facts voiced. The words extracted from a discourse, and collected together, create a personification of the self through the others; at the same time these words, gathered in the space of a notebook, provoke a crossed line of your self and the self of the others.

During the five days of working in the Dirty Ear Forum I wrote sixteen pages of notes. I did it while listening to others talk. And I did it in two specific places in Lisbon: within an art gallery in the heart of the city, and in a room of a Baroque palace.[1]

Both places affected the way in which I listened.
Both places affected me in how I listened to the others.

(~)

The space of the gallery, a standard white cube, was superimposed with some leftovers on the walls and in the storage room. These remains of a previous activity connected the alleged neatness of a gallery in Lisbon with the dirtiness of the city and the marks and traces of human activity on it. Listening in that place was looking for the otherness to happen, was dealing with the points of affection of the others, of the city, of my colleagues into my own activity.

The second space (the palace) worked the other way around. After arriving whether by car listening to the driver yelling about the crazy traffic, whether by subway in a quieter experience, the room of the palace worked as an insulating chamber by being inside a polluted room with frescoes on the walls and a chandelier hanging from the ceiling. It was an almost theatrical scenery, except for the perception-scape that sneaked in through the window:

the quietness of a suburb in the foreground delineated by the industrial activity of the sea in the background.

Looking and listening through the window was an opportunity to release the affection caused by that place. The sounds and noises, the images, the movements and also the warm air of the city, all that coming into the room through the window while I was listening to the others talk, acted like viruses mutating the genes of the overheard words into something else, demanding a relationship with the outside, to be attached to the specificity of Lisbon.

Reading back my notes is then reading a self-portrait of my situated listening of the six voices participating in the Forum[2] and the spatiality of the city of Lisbon. I can recognize my own interests delineated slightly different in the words of the others. I am able to identify in those words a synthesis of some feelings and ideas, and experiences that came up while in Lisbon. I notice how my notes, extracted from their bodies talking, were inputs to move forward and think the city and the spaces of Lisbon from new directions. I somehow perceive my listening of the others affecting my own body of work.

That's why I have decided to isolate some of these notes as headings, to refer to the performance that I proposed as part of the seminar and the resulting listening piece *O que vai acima, deve vir para baixo*. I want to celebrate in this way the collective sense of this exploration that I did as part of a fieldwork seminar to think about Sound and Affect.

In the performance I went up and down (walking and running) one of the long stone stairs of Lisbon that goes up into the Barrio Alto. I did that exercise while repeating a short sentence in Portuguese *O que vai acima, deve vir para baixo* (What goes up, must go down) to refer to the physical fact of going up and down while experiencing the exhaustion of my own body. I was looking for the interaction of sound and materiality within a specific place. I was interested in exploring those aspects of the sound of my body that were not controlled by myself. I wanted to explore the fluctuations of my voice and my body, and that's why I proposed the performative scene.

O QUE VAI ACIMA, DEVE VIR PARA ABAIXO

Go up and down a hill through stairs in the street

speaking

until your voice is distorted

Then go up the stairs again

running

without speaking anymore

Go down slowly

(~)

A SOUND BODY,

WHICH IS TRANSFORMED BY THE ENVIRONMENT

(Deborah's heard voice)

Performance. Step 1

The performance lasted less than ten minutes. I had the recorder in my hand and repeated three times the act of going up and down. I started by going up and down without saying anything. Just listening to my body hitting the floor under my feet, and the friction of the clothes on my body due to the movement. While going up and down I found and approached, step-by-step, sounds and sonic events like chirping birds, people eating, a tram or people talking. Events that I only perceived as part of a space that I comprehended while walking-listening with a recorder turned on in my hand.

Listening piece. Step 1

A whole place is listened to. An ambiance is registered in the form of a spatial perception through a low bass sound that surrounds the entire recording. The sound of steps is recognizable following a steady rhythm that makes my body gradually disappear. This sound becomes an imperfect metronome that organizes, with some irregularities in its audible beat, the other sounds heard as a determined pulse.

The distances and the topography of the space are not embodied in the sound; the sonic events are lengthened in time without almost noticing the change in the volume derived from my proximity to the source. The recording is flattening the space. And however, when listened to, an image reappears of a space pierced by a body. The increasing pace of the steps while going down emphasizes my body as being part of the city.

MODES OF KNOWING. COLLAPSE OF BORDERS
(Ana's heard voice)

Performance. Step 2
The second time I repeated the action of going up and down the stairs, I repeatedly voiced the sentence "O que vai acima" while going up, "deve vir para baixo" while going down. The action was somewhat redundant, and it was evident in my voice the performance of going up and down the stairs. The slope of the ground, the length of the stairs and the physical effort of interacting with it appeared step-by-step in the fluctuation of my voice that increasingly appeared broken. The encounter of my body with the space revealed itself augmented in the listening of my voice.

HIDDEN RHYTHMS MADE PRESENT THROUGH SOUND
(Tao's heard voice)

Listening piece. Step 2
Breathing determines the rhythm of my body and my speech. The cadence of the repeated sentence varies due to the priority of my body to catch and expel

the air. When speaking, the expulsion of air through my mouth interferes with my breathing, which becomes faster as it rises and regains its rate slightly during descent. Listening reveals a tempo that refers to my body interacting with the space. It also suggests the materiality of the stones, of the stairs, of the ground as having the potential to transform my presence there. Listening uncovers variations in the volume of my speech, as well as deviations in my pronunciation and sentences slightly choppy due to my shortness of breath.

OCCUPY THE SPACE
WITH THE ELEMENTS THE SPACE ITSELF IS OFFERING
(Rui's heard voice)

Performance. Step 3
The third time I repeated the exercise of going up and down I did it running while I ascended the stairs, and catching the breath while descending them very slowly. In the turning point I voiced the complete sentence "O que vai acima, deve vir para baixo", repeated also when I finished the performance at the bottom of the stairs.

Listening piece. Step 3
At this point of the listening, the audience doesn't need the spoken words. They know the sounds refer again to the act of going up and down. The audio recovers the presence of the bodily through the sound of my shoes beating faster with every step. They're quick beating although it is possible to perceive a decrease in their cadence while advancing in time. At some point, and as an effect of crossfading, my breath starts to have a presence in the listening, putting gradually the sound of the steps in the background. My breathing being increasingly heard reveals the exhaustion of my body, which is even more evident when I speak at the top of the stairs the complete sentence "O que vai acima, deve vir para baixo". The descent appears as the opposite process,

from breathing to stepping and then turn to the bodies: the soundscape, the city, the humans; all breathing almost at their regular pace. Is this the coming back to the original state? The voice appears again: "O que vai acima, deve vir para baixo". (Loop) A whole space is heard.

PRIVATE EXPERIENCE INTERRUPTED
(Brandon's heard voice)

This performance was an exercise in introspection where I practiced different attitudes of being in the city, interacting mainly with its surface. I explored a relationship with the architecture and the ground as materials that produce experiences beyond them. Reflecting as well on the modes by which gentrification processes transform the spaces of a city, the surfaces mainly, without going deep into the complex systems involved in them, which captures the specificity of any single place.

By walking, talking and running, I explored a contact with the space through my voice and breath being affected by four bodies: the body of architecture, the body of the soundscape, my own body in that particular place and the body of listening; having all of them the faculty of affect and also of being affected. I tried to separate myself in this way from the social space I usually work with and develop a private experience alien to it, so that I could investigate the notions of Sound and Affect beyond the social.

However, I realize that the outer, the social and the common experiences were introduced before the beginning of the performance through my decision to explore and perform in the public space while documenting the process. As well as when I decided to make a listening piece out of that performance.

What is heard was determined by the technological properties of the components of my recorder. A digital ear that listened to some sounds better than others, being the sonic result a discrimination-accentuation of the actions that happened while I was moving across the stairs. My device registered events that occurred in the spatial range of its microphone. And in doing so it flattened the space. The result resembles a cartography marked by the sound line that describes the action of going up and down the stairs. A cartography where the social fabric is materialized in the archive of relational sounds contained within it.

As I was pointing out at the beginning of this text, as listeners we select and differentiate sounds while listening. We gather them again and give them a self-meaning depending on our own experience. I wonder what assemblages of sounds and experiences listeners will develop when listening to *O que vai acima, deve vir para baixo*. Might I refer to them as forms of performativity of Sound and Affect?

(LOOP)*

*Back to the beginning

Notes:
1. The venues for the Dirty Ear Forum were the Boavista Municipal Gallery and the Palácio Pancas Palha, hosted by Companhia Olga Roriz.
2. Ana Pais, Brandon LaBelle, Deborah Kapchan, Tao G. Vrhovec Sambolec, Rui Costa and María Andueza

THE IN-BETWEEN LISTENER

RUI COSTA

Sound is a fold in the dictionary of stable certainties.

Sound can be an intimate, subtle, contingent, and specific language allowing a meaningful approach to the world.

And I like those languages that provide a sincere and empathetic communication with places, communities, psychological states, memories, ideas and ideals.

And for that to happen maybe sound is not enough for me and I should be digging meanings – ancient and forgotten meanings.

I like to think of the listener as an in-between being, a mediator, a connector.

A listener is sometimes unhappy for not belonging to what he/she listens.

A listener sometimes is happy to be able to live many lives through what he/she listens.

The act of listening to and recording a specific context or subject can be understood as a complex system of decisions, responsibilities and moralities that are primarily individual.

That is, I understand listening as a revelation mechanism that is subtle, contingent, unstable, prone to error, and primarily derived from individual perceptions.

I feel that in these fast-paced, ultra-visual, and loud times – silence, perseverance, and humility towards the specific contexts and subjects I'm working in/with can be necessary and radical acts.

How can I think, document, and creatively express specific contexts in a way

that contributes with relevant values, avoiding over-representing and over-ide-
alizing them?

I would like to lower the expectations and the ambition of both questions
through a radical process of 'context and contingency' in which I put all involved variables (the artist, the sound, the idea, the practice, the place, the
people, the expectation, the mediation, etc.) in a prism of extreme uncertainty
and fragility.

In other words, I hope that the meeting between a listener / artist and a local
context can be the least rigid and predictable as possible, precisely because
one of the counter-values of local contexts is (still) the distance towards global certainties and optimisms.

It is in the potential value of unlikely encounters that we can untie the Gord-
ian knot of this set of complex dualities that the artistic practice puts in dis-
cussion (artist / community, local / global, perennial / ephemeral, manual /
intellectual, work / art, rational / irrational, understanding / misunderstanding,
right / wrong, etc.).

While contributing with 'context and contingency' to the relationship between
sound and place, I try to propose the idea of place as a system of infinite possibilities for sound work.

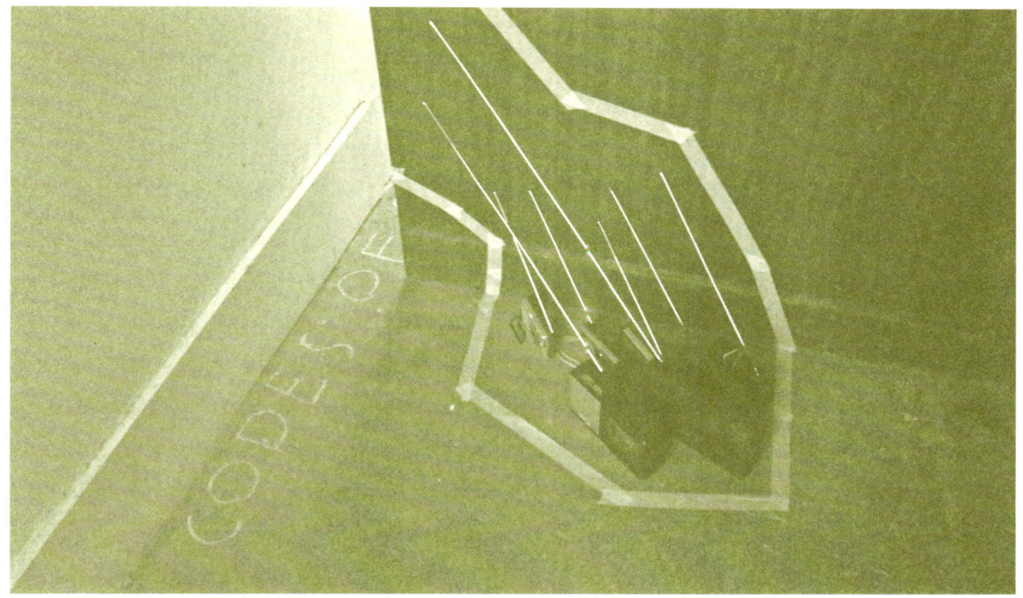

Notes on Codes of Affect, installation by Rui Costa at Dirty Ear final exhibition.

The inspiration to this piece came after a group visit to the Aljube Museum in downtown Lisbon with all the participants of Dirty Ear. Aljube was a prison that existed in the same spot since the Middle Ages, and was used during the Estado Novo dictatorship [1926 to 1974] as a political prison. Its location in one of the many old quarters of the city, across the street from the Lisbon cathedral, makes it a paradoxical place. Inmates in solitary confinement, isolated and sensory deprived against the hustle and bustle of city life. An account by a former political prisoner speaks of the sonic traces of the city that could be perceived from the cells: young girls singing popular songs in a nearby alley and the sound of transistor radios at maximum volume during the news hour or a Sunday afternoon soccer match.

Inmates would communicate with their next cell neighbors using a rudimentary code of taps on the wall: one tap for "A", two taps for "B" and so on. News about other inmates would spread using this means of communication.

Full narration of movies and political discussions would also be done throughout the night using this "impossible" code. But since there was time to spare, perhaps duration was not an issue.

The installation tried to create a confined space of bodily presence. A small and dimly lit nook in the art gallery was the chosen location. A cluster of transistor radios tuned to an FM transmission of taps on the wall occupied a corner of the installation space, with their antennae pointed towards a small passage way as if to show the way out. The radio here is not the aural glimpse of the outside world that could be overheard from inside the prison, but rather an aural trace of a reality almost unimaginable nowadays, lost in the distant past and in the faint memories of the few who endured it and are still alive.

In this installation I tried to put into practice a poetic transformation of selected elements of a specific time and place that signal the individual struggle – the psychological effect and sensorial affect of confinement – into an art piece in which the materials were organized in a discrete, fragile and open-ended way. This was a piece where reality was filtered though the lenses of individual lived experiences, and of an individual and contingent reading of those experiences. In a way, this piece tried to imagine the inner pain of each individual inmate without the presumption of knowing anything or making any definitive statement about the socio-political context of that time.

[a poem]

imprisoned tongues, free ears
eating glass so not to speak, expressive knuckles fill in the gaps
affect flows, crossing walls in impossible codes
toc-toc-toc-toc-toc
toc-toc-toc-toc-toc-toc-toc-toc-toc-toc-toc-toc-toc-toc-toc-toc-toc-toc-toc
toc-toc-toc-toc-toc-toc-toc-toc-toc-toc-toc-toc-toc-toc-toc-tqc-toc-toc-toc
toc-toc-toc-toc-toc-toc-toc-toc-toc-toc-toc-toc-toc-toc-toc
toc-toc-toc-toc-toc-toc-toc-toc-toc-toc-toc-toc-toc-toc-toc-toc-toc-toc-toc-
toc-toc

toc
toc-toc-toc-toc-toc-toc-toc-toc-toc-toc-toc-toc-toc-toc-toc-toc-toc
toc-toc-toc-toc-toc-toc-toc-toc-toc-toc-toc-toc-toc-toc-toc-toc-toc-toc-toc-
toc-toc
toc-toc-toc-toc-toc-toc-toc-toc-toc
– estou aqui [am here]

SECOND CULTURE

BRANDON LABELLE

I. Doors

It was only recently that I remembered this photograph:

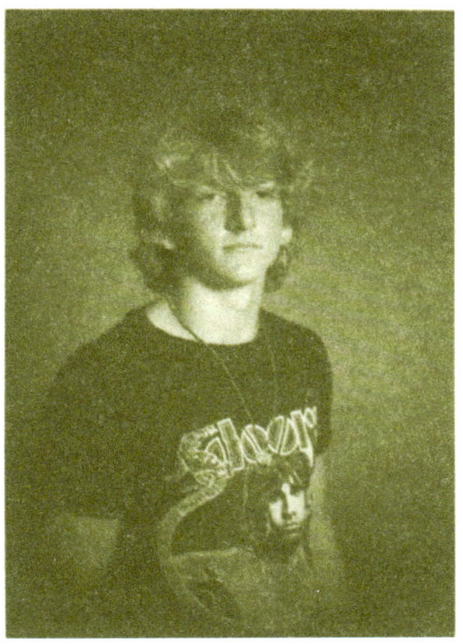

I can distinctly recall how important this day was; it is a day marked by self-determination and rebelliousness, as well as by hope in the future – hope in what I as an emerging subject confronting the social order around me might become. The photograph says: I look into the camera, not with a hard stare but instead, with a rather lost expression; I am surrendering not to the situation, but to something beyond the scene; I am transfixed by the horizon that I am beginning to see: the horizon of broken dreams, of frustrated thoughts, of longing as well as possibility, intimacy, transformation; a future that is only starting to appear, one occupied by different voices and languages: on one side, the voices of negation and of lawfulness, of ordering and prescription, and the other, a language of dreaming and of imagination and the voices that speak through the night and with the tones of freedom: in other words, on this day, when I sit still for the photograph, I begin to express myself as a subject, looked upon by so many others, and yet also, and importantly, defined by a horizon to come.

Here, I want to draw attention to an important, if not essential element; on this day, staring into the camera, the institutional framework of school life, and the social order I am beginning to confront, here, I decide to wear a particular T-shirt, one that is clearly marked by a musical reference: I look into the camera, not with a hard stare, but rather, with a lost expression – an expression which says: I am listening to a world over and above this one. The T-shirt announces, it speaks for all to see that this body, this subject is captured and is surrendering and is driven by what it listens to; it is self-determination expressed by way of the sonic imagination.

II. Night

I remember how important empty fields, abandoned sites, the cliffs and the beach, as well as pathways that crossed in and out of the light – how these were vital to being a teenager. Growing up in Southern California I was fortunate enough to be part of a small group of friends whose desires and imaginations echoed my own; in short, we were generally aligned with what others would call the drop outs, the trouble makers, and the dreamers – teenagers who were captured by existential literature, punk music, the golden sun, and landscapes of the night. In this situation, we found ourselves at odds with the normative patterns of the social milieu to a point where we often had to run, to escape, searching for alternative territories. We found such territories in the empty fields, the abandoned sites, the cliffs and the beach – edges – and upon hidden pathways that trailed over and through hills and back alleys: in a sense, we mapped out a hidden geography, criss-crossing the articulation of streets, connecting points of secret meeting between our homes, the school with trajectories of escape; we hid things in bushes, we kept clothes in trees; we knew where the cops were, and where the parents would be; and we kept to the darkness, often spending nights listening to the ocean, and to each other.

The darkness in which things may find refuge;

The darkness in which to imagine other worlds;
The darkness in which life and love found new possibilities, undercover
and out of sight;
The darkness of shared listening.

I describe these landscapes of the night, as well as that of listening, to consider how such qualities – of vacancy and periphery, of dark murmurings and whispered voices – how these afford important and rather urgent conditions for alternative sociality – a space for a second life. It is clear that without these landscapes life would have been much less bearable or edifying; I wonder, on some level, if I would have learned what it meant to be different, and how to resist the push toward conformity; what it meant to nurture loving relationships outside the family structure; and what sound and listening may help create, especially as a means of negotiation between oneself and the world. Such lessons are radically linked to peripheries, and to landscapes of the night, wherein identity can be sought outside a regime of visibility – which captured us according to our skin, our clothes, our appearance, each read as negative expressions. To stand against such discriminations required an alternative logic: a reworking of the senses and the sensible, as well as through the sharing of angst and imagining, all of which found orientation and meaning through the invisible tonalities of hidden places and the noise of being together. In short, it was necessary to formulate a practice – of nocturnal gathering and sonic attunement, and to craft a speech of and through difference.

I tell this story to situate us within a particular territory, one tensed between landscapes of the night and those of industrious life; between alternative identities and the articulation of a productive appearance; and finally, between being looked upon, watched, and a desire for the noises that might obliterate all that stood over us.

The noise, and the listening; the audible intensities that would weave together a small group of friends, undercover and out of sight, and that forms into a type of second culture: it was here, in this condition of reorientation, guided by the blue black of night and the rhythmic ocean, and from which a listening beyond what held us and toward each other took shape, that something else became possible: the making of a tribal relation, an imaginary logic.

III. Second

What might we hear in this situation now? Do we create another type of collectivity here, one also determined by listening? By a desire to reorient ourselves through other forms of knowing? Is this not a landscape, or at least a space, in which some gather? To attend to particular sounds: us, as well as the whispers and the shouts of the global order always nearby, the languages that search for other social meanings, and which capture our listening? Is there a territory nearby, or one to be constructed in which all the disenfranchised, the hopeful, the lost and the restless may gather? And which also resists my gaze?

I would say, these are questions that I carry with me, and that lead to other journeys and territories, other landscapes in which commonality may be built from the urgency of differences, and that may foster other types of self-determination, collectivity, and a shared belief in what is still possible.

It was when visiting Prague that I discovered the traces of just such a situation; and in particular, when I came to this building near the edges of the city center. The story leads us to this landscape, but also to the individuals who would gather here, to escape, to hide, as well as to form a second community, what Václav Benda would call "the parallel polis".

Throughout the 1970s and 80s, the struggle against the totalitarian system in Czechoslovakia led to the formation of illegal gatherings in which artists, musicians, writers, actors and other cultural figures tried to sustain a level of creative and critical activity. Many had been imprisoned; others were censored or

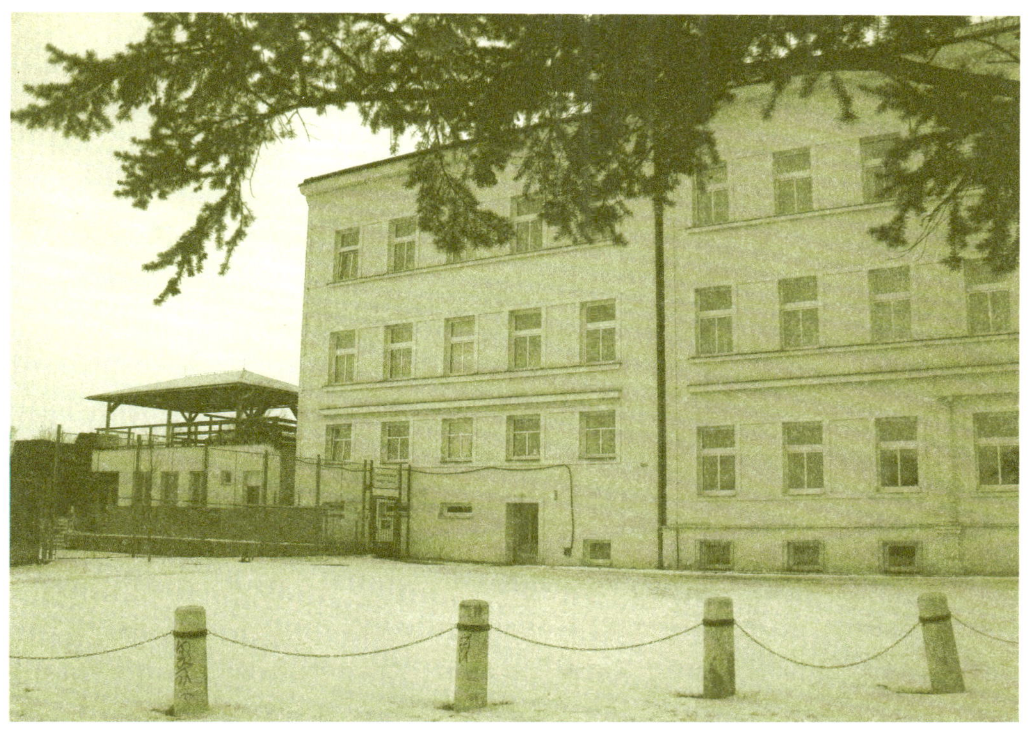

exiled. There was little room for free expression, and the possibility of openly appearing became increasingly difficult, as one could easily be criminalized, arrested. Such a condition led to attempts at resistance, as well as solidarity; to create, through desperate measures, a possible space for nurturing alternative culture. An alternative voice. The art historian Ivan Jirous would come to theorize these attempts through what he called "second culture". Second culture existed as a secret underground; gatherings and events in which certain people would come together, on the periphery, to perform and to listen together – to dream, and to resist. Within this second culture, rock and psychedelic music were a central material and reference, and Jirous himself, and others such as Václav Havel, often related the question of resistance and freedom through musical expression – finding support through the intensities of free sound. We might start to understand this as a culture founded on the sonic imagination, and a listening from below:

Ivan Jirous stands up and says:

Mystic fortunes of this otherworldly desire;

The glow and the brash resonance;

This flight of the imagination, that may tattoo the skin with languages of

loss and renewal, the fragment and then the vibration –

Shall we cry out, join together, love the streets and the dirty river?

Shall we quote the lyric, to send shivers down the spines of everyone?

This that is nowhere and everywhere;

That is inside and out;

That dips and drops, rises so high and dissipates into the ether of heav-

enly capture;

Drunk and despairing, but at least, hanging on;

And then the song picks up, continues, to vibrate the floors and the walls; making our hair stand on end, and the hands to swell with such energy – can we grab hold of all this material around us to craft a new relation, the spaces of all this life, and to escape, to crawl past the fences, hiding together, touching, whispering?

Undercover, and gathering together; a territory of survival, as well as threadbare freedom, and which I may pose as the basis for an acoustic ecology of the oppressed. There are two defining features I may highlight here: secrecies supported through the invisible and ephemeral qualities of sound and listening; and the disruptive intensities of noise, which may act as a type of weapon: to give forceful meaning to the hidden sphere and those that occupy its weak territories.

When visiting Prague, I also came upon another story told by a man I had met: he spoke of the secret musical events and the underground culture; but he also spoke of smaller, more intimate gatherings, based upon listening to illegal records smuggled in from the West. For instance, he told of how a record by the Rolling Stones became a shared object, passed from hand to hand, illegal and undercover, to be played secretly in bedrooms and backrooms, for a few gathered friends, who would listen, together. He spoke of this, and I started to imagine the scene: the coming together around this special object; spinning, sounding; the closing of doors, and of windows; closing, and the secrecy and the enthusiasm, and the withdrawal – back, back, under – within which some would find each other: identities shaped by the grooves that spiral inward, spinning, sounding; magnetized by this sonic imagination; and then out, outward, to gain intensity within this small shelter of shared excitement, angst, disillusion, and hope, undercover and in the dark, yet amplified: a second culture under the first. A second listening.

ABACULUS (LISBOA POEM)

DEBORAH KAPCHAN

I.

side walks   narrow tesserae
cobbled stones   echoing
each laid with fingers
        one next to one   carved by
                              the poorly paid

        calceteiro
        workers   of kaolinite
                                 claystone
                                 limestone
                                 shale
polished by leather
            soles   walking

gazing down where
        steps land   landing

uneven reflections   blinding

(of) the eye   (of) Lisbon

II.

cobbled stones will not stay still
they spill down the city hills
    falling one over one
    though so slowly they seem immobile
reaching up to palpate
      the soft membranes
      that trickle down their faces:
        humans living / dying
   in the time it takes to sigh

María Andueza is an artist and researcher interested in sound practices in the public sphere. She is professionally devoted to educational, cultural and artistic projects and is the initiator of Augmented Spatiality, a research platform that aims to create a flexible space for practical and theoretical investigations of public sound art based on collaboration and dialogical practices. She holds a PhD from the Complutense University of Madrid where she is now Assistant Professor in the Faculty of Fine Arts. She additionally collaborates at Museo Reina Sofía in Madrid on the radio podcast RRS as well as in other projects linked to the Education Department.

Rui Costa is a sound artist and arts programmer from Lisbon, Portugal. He is a founding member of Binaural/Nodar, an arts organization created in 2004 dedicated to the promotion of context-specific and participatory art projects in rural communities of Viseu, Portugal. Rui has been performing and exhibiting his art work since 1998 and collaborating regularly with the American intermedia artist Maile Colbert. He co-edited the book *Three Years in Nodar: Context-Specific Art Practices in Rural Portugal*, published by Edições Nodar in 2011.

Deborah Kapchan is Professor of Performance Studies at New York University. A Guggenheim fellow, she is the author of *Gender on the Market: Moroccan Women and the Revoicing of Tradition* (1996), *Traveling Spirit Masters: Moroccan Music and Trance in the Global Marketplace* (2007), as well as numerous articles on sound, narrative and poetics. Other works include *Intangible Rights: Cultural Heritage in Transit* (2014); *Theorizing Sound Writing* (2017); and *Poetic Justice: An Anthology of Moroccan Contemporary Poetry* (2019).

Brandon LaBelle is an artist and writer working with sound culture, voice, and questions of agency. He develops and presents artistic projects and performances within a range of international contexts, often working collaboratively and in public. Works include "The Other Citizen", CTM, Berlin (2019), "The

Autonomous Odyssey", Kunsthall 3,14, Bergen (2018), "The Floating Citizen", Tenerife Espacio de las Artes (2018), "The Ungovernable", Documenta 14, Athens (2017), "Oficina de Autonomia", Ybakatu, Curitiba (2017), and "The Living School", South London Gallery (2016). He is the author of *Sonic Agency: Sound and Emergent Forms of Resistance* (2018), *Lexicon of the Mouth: Poetics and Politics of Voice and the Oral Imaginary* (2014), *Diary of an Imaginary Egyptian* (2012), *Acoustic Territories: Sound Culture and Everyday Life* (2010), and *Background Noise: Perspectives on Sound Art* (2006). He lives in Berlin and is Professor at the Art Academy, University of Bergen.

Ana Pais is a FCT postdoctoral fellow at CET – Centro de Estudos de Teatro at the School of Arts and Humanities of the University of Lisbon, dramaturge and curator. She is the author of *The Discourse of Complicité. Contemporary Dramaturgies* (O Discurso da Cumplicidade. Dramaturgias Contemporâneas, Colibri, 2004) and *Affective Rhythms in the Performing Arts* (Ritmos Afectivos nas Artes Performativas, Colibri, 2018). She edited the volume *Performance na Esfera Pública* (Orfeu Negro, 2017) and its ebook version in English *Performance in The Public Sphere*, CET-Performativa, 2018) available at www.performativa. pt. She has worked as theatre critic in the most distinguished Portuguese newspapers, as a dramaturge in both theatre and dance projects in Portugal, as a lecturer at Escola Superior de Teatro e Cinema, and as curator of several discursive practice events, such as "Projecto P!" (10-14th April 2017, Lisbon).

Tao G. Vrhovec Sambolec is an Amsterdam-based artist with a particular focus in sound, new media, real-time interaction, and questions of contemporary mediation in relation to the sense of (bodily) presence. His recent work consists of spatial and sound installations, events and interventions, where (un) mediated sonic events act as central element that affectively evokes human bodily presence, while signaling its physical absence. His works have been presented internationally at various museums, galleries, project spaces and contemporary art biennales and festivals. In 2010 his work was awarded at Ars Electronica Festival in Linz – Austria.

The Dirty Ear Forum is an experimental platform for sonic research and practices, and aims to position sound as a conceptual framework that allows for experimental modes of collective work. Launched in 2013 in Berlin, the Forum is a mobile project taking place in different locations and settings, and is based on bringing together groups of practitioners to share and develop research on sound and listening. Central to the Forum is a focus on moving from singular creation to collective work, developing a common space from which a set of sonic concepts can be investigated together. This includes an engagement with new methodologies in fieldwork, experiments in sonic production, and reflections on questions of collaboration, community, horizontality and sharing. By bringing together individual viewpoints and practices into a shared activity, emphasis is placed on how sound and listening may enable the crafting of an ethics of encounter central to common life. Each Forum is guided by collective decision-making and self-organizing principles, and aims to enrich understandings of sound as an artistic, participatory, and social medium.

DIRTY EAR REPORT #3 / Errant Bodies Press, Berlin 2020 / www.errantbodies.org /
Design: fliegende Teilchen, Berlin / Print: Pinguin Druck, Berlin / ISBN: 978-0-9978744-4-0